DATE DUE		
FEB 9 2004		
JUN 1 6 2004		
AUG 3 2004		
AUG 3 0 2004		
MAY 2 3 200		

THE LIBRARY STORE   #47-0120

The Star-Spangled Banner

The Star-Spangled Banner

WRITTEN BY Amy Winstead

ILLUSTRATED BY Bob Dacey AND Debra Bandelin

ISBN 0-8249-5462-9

Published by Ideals Children's Books

An imprint of Ideals Publications

A division of Guideposts

535 Metroplex Drive, Suite 250

Nashville, Tennessee 37211

www.idealsbooks.com

Text Copyright © 2003 by Amy Winstead

Art Copyright © 2003 by Bob Dacey and Debra Bandelin

10.17/6.95 Ingram

46557   12/03

Color separations by Precision Color Graphics, Franklin, Wisconsin

Printed and bound in Italy

Library of Congress CIP data on file

10 9 8 7 6 5 4 3 2 1

Book and Cover Design by Eve DeGrie

This book is dedicated to my mother, Etta Wilson, who shared the love of children's literature with me and encouraged me as a writer. AW

In memory of Richard Huebner. BD

To my son, John. DB

Oh say can you see, by the dawn's early light,

What so proudly we hail'd at the twilight's last gleaming . . .

JED McTAVISH LIKED HELPING his older brother Nathan on their father's oyster boat. The boys had worked alone since their dad had joined the Maryland Militia.

Early every morning they sailed out from the Baltimore harbor, past Fort McHenry with its big flag flying above the fort. Most evenings, the boys returned home with a large catch of oysters which they would sell quickly. America was at war with Britain, and American soldiers were hungry.

One September morning, Jed and Nathan had just raised their first catch of oysters when Jed saw British warships sailing toward the fort. He was frightened. The newspapers were full of reports about fishermen being seized by British sailors. Worse than that, the British had burned the United States Capitol in Washington. Were they now heading toward Baltimore?

"Nathan, look! British ships!" Jed called out.

"Quick, run up the sail!" yelled Nathan.

But it was too late. A British rowboat was headed for the boys.

"Halt!" shouted one of the British sailors. "In the name of the king, we are seizing your boat."

"He's no king of mine!" Jed called back.

"You're a real Yankee Doodle, aren't you?" the sailor said with a sneer.

When the British boat came close, Jed saw four sailors at the oars. A soldier guarded three men seated in the middle of the boat.

The British sailors pulled their boat close to the boys' boat.

"Climb aboard, boys," the British navy officer shouted. "You can join these Americans on that truce ship that lies anchored over there. For now, you must watch as the king's navy captures Fort McHenry. It won't be long."

"It may take longer than you think!" said one of the prisoners.

The British sailors motioned the boys into the crowded rowboat.

As Jed climbed into the boat, one of the prisoners smiled at Jed and said, "Greetings, young man. What's your name?"

"Jed, sir, and this is my brother Nathan."

"My name is Francis Scott Key, and these gentlemen are Dr. Beanes and Colonel Skinner."

"Do you know what the British will do to us?" asked Jed.

"Don't be afraid," Mr. Key said. "Colonel Skinner and I have been aboard the British flagship to secure the release of Dr. Beanes. The admiral freed him but will not allow us to return home until after the battle."

"Do the British intend to attack Baltimore?" asked Jed.

"Yes," replied Mr. Key. "We must hope and pray that the flag over Fort McHenry still flies in the morning."

The British boat delivered the Americans to the deck of a small ship that lay behind the British warships.

Boom! Jed jumped as the first cannon shot roared from a British ship. Immediately, the cannons at Fort McHenry fired back, but their shots fell short of the British ships. The Americans would have a hard battle ahead.

The British ships kept firing as the sun sank behind the fort. When the sky grew dark, the red glare of rockets swept through the night sky. The sound was so loud, Jed knew no one in Baltimore would sleep that night.

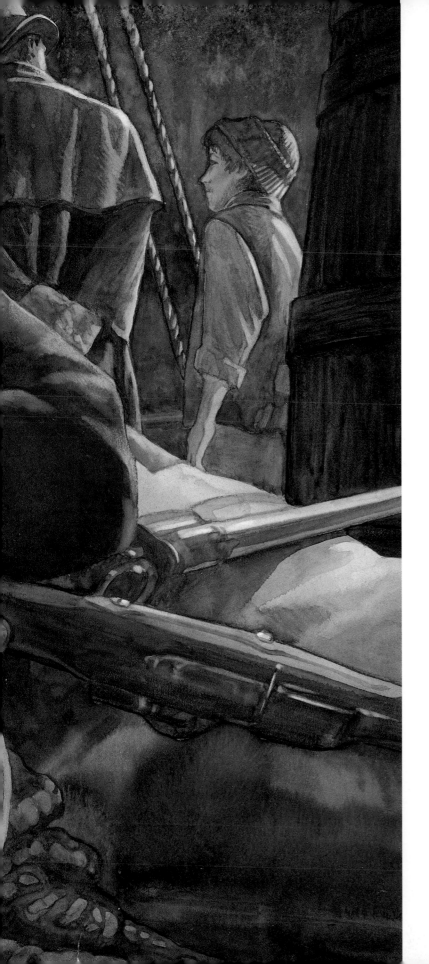

Boom! . . . Boom! . . . Boom!
Hour after hour, the cannons roared
and rockets lit up the sky. Nathan
curled up on the deck and went to
sleep. The British guards were also
napping, their muskets at their sides.

Mr. Key paced the deck and
watched each rocket as it burst in the
air. Jed followed him, step by step.

"Where is your father, young
man?" asked Mr. Key.

"He is serving his country with
the Maryland Militia."

"He was serving also with the
oysters he supplied to the troops,"
Mr. Key said with a smile.

"Yes, sir, but my father knows
the harbor better than anyone. He
had many discussions with the fort's
commander about sinking ships in the
harbor. These ships now underwater
will keep the British ships away from
shore."

"A daring plan, and it may save
the city tonight," said Mr. Key.

About dawn the next morning, the British guns fell silent. Mr. Key leaned over the rail and turned his spyglass toward the fort.

"Our flag, Jed. I can still see it, even through the fog and smoke!"

Jed leaped up. "Where? Does it still fly?"

Mr. Key handed Jed his spyglass and pointed toward the fort.

Jed looked through the glass, and the gray, rainy day seemed to brighten just a little.

"The Stars and Stripes still waves!" he shouted.

Then Jed turned to look at the British ships. They were heading out to sea, their guns empty and still. The Americans still held Fort McHenry.

Just then Dr. Beanes woke up. Mr. Key pointed toward the American flag, and Dr. Beanes let out a mighty "Hurray!" This woke up Nathan and the British guards. They looked first at the fort and then at the ships sailing away.

"You men are about to let us go free," Dr. Beanes laughed. "Or else you will spend some time in the Baltimore jail."

In the midst of the excitement, Mr. Key turned to Jed. "Do you have anything to write with?" he asked.

"Only this stick of charcoal we use to record our oyster catch each day," Jed replied.

Mr. Key pulled an old envelope from his coat pocket, sat down, and began to write. "I would like to write a poem about our great victory today."

It was noon before Jed and Nathan were back onboard their boat and had unfurled its sails. They had not caught any oysters, but they would never forget the night of September 13, 1814. Jed couldn't wait to tell his father.

A few days later, Jed and Nathan were unloading their day's catch of oysters. Jed picked up the front page of the *Baltimore Patriot* and started to wrap a dozen fresh oysters. He stopped when he saw a drawing of the American flag. Beside it, in large print, was a poem by "a gentleman of Maryland."

A big smile spread across Jed's face as he read the poem. He knew who had written those words about "the perilous fight" and "the land of the free and the home of the brave."

Quickly he folded the page, put it in his pocket, and picked up another sheet. If he ever saw Mr. Key again, he would wrap the most tender oysters of all to give to him and thank him for his poem.

THE STAR-SPANGLED BANNER

Oh say can you see, by the dawn's early light,

What so proudly we hail'd at the twilight's last gleaming,

Whose broad stripes and bright stars through the perilous fight,

O'er the ramparts we watched were so gallantly streaming?

And the rockets' red glare, the bombs bursting in air,

Gave proof through the night that our flag was still there;

Oh say does that star-spangled banner yet wave,

O'er the land of the free, and the home of the brave?